THE ICELANDIC
*H*ORSE
in the Home Country

THE ICELANDIC
HORSE
in the Home Country

Iceland Review

Text © Jóhanna S. Sigthórsdóttir 1996
Photography: Páll Stefánsson
English translation: Gary Gunning
Design: Gudjón Sveinbjörnsson
Printed in Singapore
Published by Iceland Review ©, Reykjavík, Iceland 1996

ISBN 9979-51-107-9

Introduction

The Icelandic horse has from the beginning played a crucial role in Icelandic society, and the breed's history is inextricably intertwined with that of the country and nation. This small-statured and tough breed has not only been a diligent servant of man throughout the centuries, but has also been a true friend and companion. The Icelandic horse has earned the respect and affection of people in many countries and its popularity is steadily increasing.

Particular reasons behind the breed's popularity are its mastery of so many gaits, its agility and gentleness, its strength and industriousness. The breed possesses all the qualities of an untamed animal of nature, but is nonetheless docile and easily managed.

It is almost certain that the immediate ancestral roots of the breed lie in Norway. Viking-Age horse skeletons which have been unearthed in Iceland support the hypothesis that the Icelandic horse is descended from Norwegian imports. These skeletal remains have been compared with the bones of Norwegian horses from the same period, and are remarkably similar in size and build.

The efforts of scientists have further shown that the Icelandic horse has varied in size over the centuries. The cur-

rent average height for the breed is 13.1 hands. This average height has grown rapidly in the past ten to fifteen years as breeders have, amongst other things, sought to produce larger horses. Market forces have also played a role in increasing the size of the breed, larger animals having proved easier to sell than their smaller counterparts. Breeders and fans of the Icelandic horse have, however, been on the alert lest the increase in size should detract from the breed's distinctive characteristics. The current consensus among observers is that an optimal height for the Icelandic horse has now been achieved.

The following pages aim to present a picture of the Icelandic horse in the home country – to show his unique character and numerous qualities, and describe the conditions with which the breed has lived in the past and under which it today thrives.

Small but Adaptable

Due to its diverse qualities, the Icelandic horse is considered unique by equine enthusiasts the world over. Perhaps more surprising is that the breed has been exceptionally well preserved, just as the integrity of the Icelandic language has been zealously guarded.

It was the first Viking settlers who brought the horse with them to Iceland some eleven centuries ago, and the breed has since maintained its special characteristics. Breeds on the European mainland, however, have undergone extensive mixing and cross-breeding. There are currently about 80,000 horses in Iceland.

The Icelandic horse is small and stocky, and his environment, his various roles through the centuries and his physique have produced an animal renowned for strength, surefootedness and stamina. These qualities have ensured that the Icelandic horse has become very popular abroad. Among the countries where breeding of the Icelandic horse has flourished are: Germany, the Scandinavian lands, the UK, Austria, France, Holland and Switzerland. The breed has also been successfully introduced in the US and Canada.

The Spirit of Spring

Recent years have seen a phenomenal expansion in the breeding and export of the Icelandic horse. There has also been an accompanying rise in the number of Icelanders employed in taming, training, selling and shipping the horses to foreign buyers. It is thus no wonder that since horse breeding has become an established sector in Icelandic agriculture, the number of horses has steadily increased in Iceland.

An inspiring sight that often greets travellers in Iceland in the spring months is the spectacle of large herds of horses slowly moving across the grasslands. As the adults seek out choice pastures, the young horses can be seen playing and sporting in the fields.

Experienced horsemen in Iceland believe that the first days of a foal's life show how the animal will be as a mature horse. The foal's movements indicate the extent of the horse's gaits, and show whether the horse will have the high-stepping *tölt* (running walk) gait or the more prosaic *brokk* (trot).

A Traditional Gift

The histories of man and horse in Iceland have been inextricably linked ever since the ninth-century settlement. According to old stories and sources the horse was highly regarded by the settlers, even to the extent that a slain warrior was often buried alongside his mount. Some of the early Icelanders imparted a religious significance to horses, while no gift was as welcome and esteemed as a good horse. Even kings were given horses if the occasion was thought auspicious enough. The tradition lives on, for when the Crown Princess Margarethe of Denmark was married in 1967, the Icelandic nation gave her a pair of fully outfitted breeding mares. Horses were also thought the most appropriate reward for deeds of rescue, and there are examples of the animal being given as a benefice to churches.

Old historical records tell of chieftains crossing their territory on horseback, some on peaceful missions, others intent on violence and bloody feuds with their enemies. The events from this period of Iceland's history live on in the Icelandic imagination, and have provided a rich source of raw material for the country's blossoming cinema industry.

An Indispensable Servant

The role of the Icelandic horse has altered dramatically in recent years. The horse was for centuries the sole means of transport and communication in Iceland, not to mention the only working animal. Before the arrival of machinery and mechanised transport, people were completely reliant on trusty and strong horses. No wonder that the horse was called the "most useful servant" by Icelanders. This dependence was highlighted in emergency situations when it was necessary to travel long distances through bad weather in search of help, a doctor or a midwife. Countless tales survive of horses who, by sheer strength and tenacity, saved human lives on such arduous journeys.

Before the motor-age, all post between the various districts of Iceland was moved by horse. As postal services had to be maintained all year round and in all conditions, those working with its transport often landed in difficulties. The widespread use of mechanisation had largely made the Icelandic horse redundant by the middle of the twentieth century. There were, however, Icelanders interested in good riding horses, and it was their coordinated efforts that forged new dignified roles for the Icelandic horse.

Destination Unknown

A pleasure for every rider of the Icelandic horse is to set off on his mount on a beautiful summer's evening, and as the sun dips towards the horizon, to ride into the unknown. There is no rush, as Icelandic summer nights are as bright as the days. At such moments man and horse are one, sprightly feet dance across the soft earth and each step is a praise to life. One Icelandic farmer has aptly described his mount as a "dancing sanctity."

The Icelandic horse brings out man's joy for life, and nowhere is a horseman more likely to break out into song than sitting astride his mount – it is not without reason that riding an Icelandic horse is often likened to "poetry in motion."

Born Free

What helps explain the famed special characteristics of the Icelandic horse is the freedom he enjoys. Herds are kept behind fences on large areas of ground where they can run unhindered. A distinctly Icelandic panorama of mountains, glaciers, hills and pastures is constantly before the horses' eyes. The freedom in which the Icelandic horse grows up is shown in his behaviour. He is attentive, closely attuned to his environment and temperament.

This grazing pasture at the foot of Snæfellsjökull glacier is typical of the environment which Mother Nature offers the Icelandic horse. This is his home.

Legendary Creatures

There exists in the minds of Icelanders an unbreakable bond between horses and water, a bond that dates from the settlement right up to the present day. Legends and stories mention a fantastic creature of horselike appearance, the *nykur*, which dwelt in lakes. The mysterious *nykur* was generally grey in colour and its hooves and fetlocks were turned back to front.

The medieval Book of Settlements relates one incident in the "history" of the *nykur*: a settler by the name of Audun Stoti had taken the land around Hraunsfjördur, and one autumn he saw an apple grey horse run from Hjardarvatn lake towards his herd of stallions. The grey intruder then began to fight and eventually overcame one of Audun's horses which was standing guard over the stallions. The courageous Audun seized the newcomer, set him before a cart meant for two oxen, and set off for home with all his hay. The horse was at first easy to manage, but as the day wore on he began to plough and scrape up the earth with his hooves. When the sun had set the horse slipped its bridle and ran to the lake. It was never seen again.

A High Point for Horsemen

*R*iding trips in Iceland are enjoying increasing popularity. And it's no surprise, for a definite high point for any horseman is a lengthy riding trip, either alone or in groups.

It is on such rides that one gets to know one's mount and his potential, and also to learn about the horse's temperament and qualities. The horse, too, learns what kind of a master he has. Long riding trips are an ideal opportunity for rider and mount to really become acquainted with each other.

Kjölur, an old roadway in the Icelandic hinterland, has a special appeal for the modern horseman. Beginning in the south, the route takes riders right across the country between Hofsjökull and Langjökull glaciers, and on to Hveravellir before ending in Skagafjördur in north Iceland. The Kjölur route allows the traveller to view Iceland's landscape in all its spectacular beauty: scenes ranging from lush pastures to semi-desert wastes. This ancient roadway has also been the scene of some of the most demanding and glorious journeys ever undertaken by man and horse in Iceland.

Making a Friend

Recent years have seen an explosion in the numbers of foreign visitors coming to Iceland solely on account of the Icelandic horse. Thousands of overseas guests now travel annually to Iceland to take part in tournaments, go on riding trips and experience the Icelandic horse in his natural environment. This upsurge in foreign interest has generated considerable employment for Icelanders engaged in organising and providing riding tours.

Many tourists go so far as to buy horses on such visits to Iceland. Some visitors have decided on their purchase beforehand, and one of the purposes of coming to Iceland is to choose a beautiful horse from the large herds of touring mounts.

Other tourists become enchanted with a particular horse and simply cannot imagine returning home without their discovery. The decision to buy an Icelandic horse is a big step, both for the new overseas owner and the horse, as once a horse has left Iceland it may never return. The imposed exile on exported horses is due to stringent disease control regulations, and such drastic measures have ensured that the Icelandic horse is free of infectious ailments that afflict other breeds.

Navigating Fords

In bygone days there were no bridges across rivers in Iceland, and the only alternative was to cross them by horseback. Many of the rivers were extremely difficult to cross as they were often deep, fast-flowing bodies of glacial water. The only means of traversing such rivers was by travelling across fords. Local guides with expert knowledge were also called upon to show travellers the safest crossing points. Time and again travellers had to cross these rivers atop a horse.

On account of such hazardous conditions, horses from particular localities were considered more trustworthy than others for river crossings. Traditionally valued for their courage and sure-footedness when negotiating rivers were horses from Hornafjördur in southeast Iceland. Horses from this district were accustomed from an early age to bearing their owners across raging glacial rivers such as the Jökulsá river and the Skeidará river in the east of the country.

Winning Trust

Good interplay between horse and rider is necessary if the animal's qualities are to be used to their best. Thus the horse-breaker seeks to win the foal's trust at the very outset of training.

The horse is an enigma – an enigma which must be solved. This becomes obvious to a good trainer the moment he looks into the eyes of an eager horse before sitting in the saddle. Both horse and rider look forward to their time together. Slowly but surely the rider gets to know his horse, and both man and beast celebrate each step forward they make. It is crucial to maintain the horse's sense of well-being, as it is his driving will power that spurs him on to further efforts. This will power and vigour can often be seen in the horse's sparkling eyes and determined poise.

A well-known Icelandic trainer has pointed out that a horse should never be broken to the point where his distinctive characteristics are erased: the wild passion of the horse should never be destroyed, only brought under control.

A Treasury of Colours

The colours of the Icelandic horse span a wide spectrum; indeed it would appear as if they include all the basic colours and shades to be found amongst any breed of horses. So diverse is the spectrum that an individual horse may sometimes boast three primary colours, the piebald being a perfect example.

The rarest colour for the Icelandic horse is roan. No more than 200-300 examples of horses of that colour currently exist, and there are fears that the colouring may die out in the near future if special measures are not taken. Roan horses are unique in that their colouring changes with the seasons. As they shed their winter coats they turn darker: dark red, brown, bay or cream. Their coats lighten in colour however as summer progresses, and their winter coats are fair to the point of whiteness.

The silver dapple colour is also rather rare, but much sought after. Such horses are either black-brown or dark red on the belly with a silver-coloured tail and mane. Red and dark dappled horses are common, as well as grey, piebald and light clay-brown. The most common colours for the Icelandic horse are, however, red and brown, but both contain a variety of hues.

The Roundups

With the coming of spring Icelandic farmers release their sheep into mountain pastures and the remote interior. The flocks are allowed to graze undisturbed in the wild all summer, but during autumn the farmers saddle up and set out to round up their flocks.

In some areas of the country the roundup can take as long as a week, with the horsemen sheltering in huts and cabins. The roundup is undertaken by the farmers of a particular district, and all the sheep gathered are driven to a common fold for later sorting among the rightful owners.

These annual roundups are a trying time for riders, mounts and the accompanying sheepdogs. The undertaking is both a cooperative venture and a carefully coordinated effort, as anybody might land in a game of pursuit with rebellious or wary sheep. The pursuit might even drag on for a considerable period if conditions are difficult. A good roundup horse plays a full and vital role in the roundups and can be counted upon even when a farmer slings an exhausted lamb across the horse's neck. Traditionally dogs also play a crucial role in collecting the sheep, and the three partners of man, dog and horse must understand and work with one another. There is more than a grain of truth in the Icelandic saying: "A secret bond links man, horse and dog."

Horsemen's Dreams

*I*t is no doubt the dream of every horseman to someday own a horse good enough to enter at one of the big annual shows.

The Icelandic horse is an impressive sight when displaying the *tölt*, and although other breeds possess this gait, none other does it as smoothly as the Icelandic breed. Barely moving in the saddle, the rider feels the clean rhythm of the gait through a pliant foot in the stirrup.

For long it was thought that a horse was not top-rank unless he possessed all five traits, i.e. *tölt, brokk, skeid* (pace), *fetgangur* (walk or step) and *stökk* (gallop). Some horses possess great facility in the *tölt*, but are without the *skeid*, a double-paced gait in which the horse moves the two feet on each side simultaneously. In *skeid* events it is speed that is decisive, while in *tölt* shows, the horse is expected to display its handsomeness and agility.

Competitions and Exhibitions

*V*arious competitions are held at the large horse meets held in Iceland. The horses compete amongst themselves to determine which animal is best in the gaits, while stallions and mares are exhibited and individually judged on a range of traits.

Judging the qualities and traits of stallions is one of the highlights of the big meets. These competitions allow comparisons to be made between the stallions, and spectators can judge the common characteristics of groups of horses and the abilities of individual mounts.

Riders and owners go to great lengths to ensure that their stallions receive the highest scores. Groups of horses are first displayed, but then they are whittled down and individual horses are allowed to show their own particular qualities and traits. An eager buzz of excitement often runs through the rows of spectators when rider after rider launches his horse through a flying *skeid* – something many find the most impressive quality of each good horse.

National Horse Meets

*I*celandic horsemen have held quadrennial annual horse meets since 1951 and only the country's very best horses are displayed at these national events. So high is the prestige of these get-togethers that there is always keen competition within each riding club to determine which horse or horses will be picked as the club's representatives.

The selection process for the clubs' mares and stallions takes place during spring, and it is this selection which qualifies the horses for inclusion in the nationals. As only the crème de la crème of Icelandic horses survive the rigorous preliminaries, the national meets are a true embarrassment of riches for all fans of the breed.

The Sunday morning of each meet witnesses a moving ceremony as horsemen from every district of the country assemble along with their mounts and, suitably attired for the occasion, set off on a group ride under a fluttering Icelandic flag. The display is a sign of genuine respect and honour for both the Icelandic horse and his devoted supporters.

But such meets are by no means limited to Iceland. Every second year sees the World Championship of the Icelandic horse held in one of the participating countries of FEIF (The Federation of European Friends of the Icelandic Horse).

A Special Status

There is one concept which every true horseman is familiar with: a horse is inviolate and may not be touched without the owner's permission. Indeed, it has for long been considered almost a sacrilege to steal or commandeer a horse in Iceland. But this hasn't prevented the emergence of many tales about such incidents.

One particular folk tale tells of the Rev. Eiríkur in Vogsósar, a clergyman reputedly versed in magic and sorcery. The tale relates that two lively school boys came to where the priest lived and stole the good Reverend's horses. However, when the youths decided to dismount they found they were stuck fast on the horses' backs! The horses then galloped home to the rightful owner, and the priest met the returning boys. Fortunately for the boys, Rev. Eiríkur thought it punishment enough that their misdeed had been exposed.

The moral of the tale is quite clear: it simply doesn't pay to steal a horse, as the thief will sooner or later be uncovered.

The Horse and the Land

The highlands of the Icelandic interior are magnificent and virtually untouched. Such roads as exist are tracks that have been carved out over the centuries. In some regions movement is restricted to birds in the sky, while in other areas transport is only possible using the time-honoured method – the horse.

Compared to the awesome majesty of untamed nature, men and horses are mere insignificances. It is at times like these, astride a mount in Jökuldalur valley, that the rider feels dwarfed by his surroundings. The clash in proportions notwithstanding, the rider knows that together with his horse most roads are still open.

Raised in the Wild

Farmers in the Skagafjördur and Húnavatnssýsla regions in north Iceland still have the benefit of raising some of their mares and foals on moors and heaths from early summer onwards. At this time of the year the grasslands of the interior have far outstripped those of more built-up areas in terms of available pastures. The horses are kept in these districts until autumn in conditions that breeders say are ideal. The horses are kept distant from man and his influence, and the young horses learn from their environment and adjust to the rules that govern within the free-running herds. Horses from many farms are kept to the same locality, but each particular group keeps a respectful distance from the others.

The above arrangement once prevailed in south Iceland, but has been discontinued due to an increased awareness about land and soil conservation. Another practice that was allowed until approximately fifty years ago was that of allowing stallions to mix freely with mares, even many from one farm. It was thus uncertain which horse had sired which foal, although it was almost certain that the responsible stallion belonged to the same farm as the mothering mare. This could safely be assumed because the stallion kept an exceptionally sharp eye over his mares, and was swift to repulse unwelcome male competition.

Sorting out the Herds

Farmers in north Iceland round up their horses from the grasslands and interior and bring them to shelter at the same time they collect their sheep. Just like the sheep roundup, the horses are driven into large common pens where each horse is sorted and delivered to its respective owner. It often becomes somewhat rough in the pens, as the horses are touchy following their months of freedom and are sensitive to human touch. But most of the high-spirited horses are, however, quickly calmed once they have been together with man for a while.

The horse roundups in north Iceland are now one of the major attractions for horse admirers. Crowds meet not only to chat, but also to speculate on the hundreds of horses that have been gathered in one spot. Many also spot a horse that grabs their fancy, and the pens are transformed into hectic market places.

A Creation of the Almighty

Not all farmers who breed horses do so for worldly gain or out of practical considerations. Many farmers keep horses simply because they find them attractive, or are fond of them. Such breeders feel they are playing an active role in assisting one of God's wonders of creation, especially when they see the foals entering the world in spring and follow their progress in the folds.

The Atom Station, one of the best-known novels of Iceland's Nobel laureate for literature Halldór Laxness, tells of one Falur the Farmer in Eystridalur valley. It was said that this particular farmer believed in horses, and the following quotation spoken by Falur is an accurate and true representation:

"One of the loveliest and most magnificent events that can happen in the country is when ponies take fright, particularly in a herd. (...) Then all at once it is as if the fire had started flowing right under these strange creatures, they charge away like a storm incarnate over scree and bogs and landslides, dipping the tips of their toes for a fractional moment into the furnace that blazes beneath their hooves, cutting across waterfalls, gulleys, and boulders, galloping steeply for a while until they stand trapped at last on some ledge high in the mountain-tops..."

Ice Games

During the winter months the riding horses are sheltered in enclosed stables, and depending on the weather are usually kept indoors from Christmas onwards. The horses are then confined until June when they are released for summer grazing.

But even during the sometimes inclement Icelandic winter, the horses can be put to a variety of uses, some of the most popular being winter games and "ice tournaments" where riders meet with their mounts on frozen lakes and ponds. Nothing equals taking a favourite horse for an invigorating ride across crackling ice, and under the clear winter moonlight such trips can seem like a living chapter from some enchanted fairy tale. On such evenings it is truly a pleasure to be alive.

Another winter treat for horse enthusiasts is the group outings on holidays and festivals. Farmers in Fljótshlíd, south Iceland, for example, meet together for an extended ride on Easter Sunday. Such trips are especially looked forward to, as they provide a welcome break from the tough farming routine.

Winter Quarters

Breeding horses are generally kept outdoors during the winter months, and as Icelandic winters can be harsh and grass supplies meagre, farmers provide the herds with fodder.

The treatment of outdoor horses during winter has changed considerably in recent years. Whereas it was once thought sufficient to supply the horses with leftovers and refuse of hay from the sheep and cattle, breeders now strive to ensure an adequate fodder supply and decent shelter.

The Icelandic horse is well equipped to survive the trials of the winter months. Already as autumn approaches the horse changes into a special winter "outfit" as its coat thickens and the horse adopts a shaggy, long-haired appearance.

Extra reserves of fat also start appearing on the horse as winter looms, the formation, one might say, of a natural larder to see the horse through the coming lean months.

The above two tactics enable the horse to survive driving snowstorms and bitter frost, provided of course that adequate shelter and fodder have been made available.

The Homing Instinct

The Icelandic horse has long been renowned for its baffling sense of direction and unerring homing instinct. There are countless examples of horses being sold and transferred to different areas of the country only to reappear days, or even months later, at their home pastures.

One recorded incident from the turn of the last century testifies to the Icelandic horse's uncanny sense of direction. Two farmers were returning home one winter after buying provisions in the town of Húsavík in northeast Iceland. They still had a long journey ahead of them with their horses and sledge when they were suddenly engulfed by a driving blizzard and plummeting temperatures. The farmers were soon quite lost and had no idea of their location. Driven by desperation the men decided to unhitch one of the horses in order to let him guide the way out of the storm. The horse of course led the way and was soon plotting a course that was the exact opposite of the route the men would have taken! After a long journey the horse finally led the exhausted farmers to a sheep hut, thus saving their lives.

"The Horse Laugh"

Horses are as temperamentally individual as their owners, and each animal has his own peculiar characteristics that are no doubt inherited but also moulded by upbringing and environment. A horse's inner character can often be perceived by observing his bearing and behaviour. Such traits as eye colour, the shape of the ears, neighing and tail movements can also provide clues to the horse's temperament. By ignoring such traits in their horses, riders may well plant the seeds for future discord between man and mount. Reason enough indeed for the expression "he laughs loudest who laughs last." It is also fitting that an unrestrained and hearty laugh is in Icelandic called *hrossahlátur* – a horse laugh.